T011000

EXODUS

GOD OUR DELIVERER

14 Studies for Individuals or Groups

DALE & SANDY LARSEN

SHAW

WATERBROOK
PRESS

Exodus
A Shaw Book
Published By WaterBrook Press
2375 Telstar Drive, Suite 160
Colorado Springs, CO 80920
A division of Random House, Inc.

ISBN: 978-0-87788-209-1

Editor: Mary Horner Collins
Cover photo © 1998 by Dick Dietrich

Printed in the United States of America

146502721

CONTENTS

INTRODUCTION

"God, get me out of this!"

How often have you said that? Are you in a situation right now that makes you say it?

When the Israelites were slaves in Egypt, they had plenty of opportunities and plenty of reasons to beg, "God, get us out of this!" They had wound up in Egypt because Joseph was sold into slavery by his own brothers. Joseph did not continue as a slave; through God's intervention and faithfulness Joseph rose to power in Egypt. Eventually Joseph's father, Israel, his brothers and their families all found refuge from famine in Egypt with him. Initially, the Israelites flourished. But later when a Pharaoh came along who knew nothing of Joseph, he saw this vast group of Hebrews as a threat and enslaved them.

The new Pharaoh may not have known about Joseph, but the Israelites knew their own history. They knew the Lord had pulled Joseph up out of humiliation, slavery, and false imprisonment. Would the Lord do it again, this time for an entire people?

In many ways we're in the same condition as the Israelites. We live under various external and internal struggles—with difficult people or situations, with our own sin and failings. We know God *can* deliver us; we know it from what we read in the Bible and have seen in our own and others' experiences. But *will* he deliver us? When? How? Is he leaving us in a difficult situation for a purpose? And what do we have to do, if anything, to help our deliverance happen?

God's deliverance comes in many different ways, as the Israelites learned. Sometimes it means miraculous rescue from trouble. Other times it means a change of heart or an internal strengthening which is equally miraculous.

So the story of the Exodus is also our story, because it is the story of God's deliverance of an imperfect people. The story doesn't always read the way we'd like. The trip is rough. Sometimes it doubles back or gets delayed. But it is always going somewhere, and most important, God is there with us at every step.

HOW TO USE THIS STUDYGUIDE

Fisherman studyguides are based on the inductive approach to Bible study. Inductive study is discovery study; we discover what the Bible says as we ask questions about its content and search for answers. This is quite different from the process in which a teacher *tells* a group *about* the Bible, what it means, and what to do about it. In inductive study God speaks directly to each of us through his Word.

A group functions best when a leader keeps the discussion on target, but this leader is neither the teacher nor the "answer person." A leader's responsibility is to *ask*—not *tell*. The answers come from the text itself as group members examine, discuss, and think together about the passage.

There are four kinds of questions in each study. The first is an *approach question*. Used before the Bible passage is read, this question breaks the ice and helps you focus on the topic of the Bible study. It begins to reveal where thoughts and feelings need to be transformed by Scripture.

Some of the earlier questions in each study are *observation questions* designed to help you find out basic facts—who, what, where, when, and how.

When you know what the Bible says, you need to ask, *What does it mean?* These *interpretation questions* help you to discover the writer's basic message.

Application questions ask *What does it mean to me?* They challenge you to live out the Scripture's life-transforming message.

Fisherman studyguides provide spaces between questions for jotting down responses and related questions you would like to raise in the group. Each group member should have a copy of the studyguide and may take a turn in leading the group.

For consistency, Fisherman guides are written from the *New International Version.* But a group should feel free to use the NIV or any other accurate, modern translation of the Bible such as the *New Living Translation,* the *New Revised Standard Version,* the *New Jerusalem Bible,* or the *Good News Bible.* (Other paraphrases of the Bible may be referred to when additional help is needed.) Bible commentaries should not be brought to a Bible study because they tend to dampen discussion and keep people from thinking for themselves.

SUGGESTIONS FOR GROUP LEADERS

1. Read and study the Bible passage thoroughly beforehand, grasping its themes and applying its teachings for yourself. Pray that the Holy Spirit will "guide you into truth" so that your leadership will guide others.

2. If the studyguide's questions ever seem ambiguous or unnatural to you, rephrase them, feeling free to add others that seem necessary to bring out the meaning of a verse.

3. Begin (and end) the study promptly. Start by asking someone to pray for God's help. Remember, the Holy Spirit is the teacher, not you!

4. Ask for volunteers to read the passages out loud.

5. As you ask the studyguide's questions in sequence, encourage everyone to participate in the discussion. If some are silent, ask,

"What do you think, Heather?" or "Dan, what can you add to that answer?" or suggest, "Let's have an answer from someone who hasn't spoken up yet."

6. If a question comes up that you can't answer, don't be afraid to admit that you're baffled! Assign the topic as a research project for someone to report on next week.

7. Keep the discussion moving and focused. Though tangents will inevitably be introduced, you can bring the discussion back to the topic at hand. Learn to pace the discussion so that you finish a study each session you meet.

8. Don't be afraid of silences; some questions take time to answer and some people need time to gather courage to speak. If silence persists, rephrase your question, but resist the temptation to answer it yourself.

9. If someone comes up with an answer that is clearly illogical or unbiblical, ask him or her for further clarification: "What verse suggests that to you?"

10. Discourage Bible-hopping and overuse of cross-references. Learn all you can from *this* passage, along with a few important references suggested in the studyguide.

11. Some questions are marked with a ♦. This indicates that further information is available in the Leader's Notes at the back of the guide.

12. For further information on getting a new Bible study group started and keeping it functioning effectively, read Gladys Hunt's *You Can Start a Bible Study Group* and *Pilgrims in Progress: Growing through Groups* by Jim and Carol Plueddemann.

SUGGESTIONS FOR GROUP MEMBERS

1. Learn and apply the following ground rules for effective Bible study. (If new members join the group later, review these guidelines with the whole group.)

2. Remember that your goal is to learn all that you can *from the Bible passage being studied.* Let it speak for itself without using Bible commentaries or other Bible passages. There is more than enough in each assigned passage to keep your group productively occupied for one session. Sticking to the passage saves the group from insecurity and confusion.

3. Avoid the temptation to bring up those fascinating tangents that don't really grow out of the passage you are discussing. If the topic is of common interest, you can bring it up later in informal conversation following the study. Meanwhile, help each other stick to the subject!

4. Encourage each other to participate. People remember best what they discover and verbalize for themselves. Some people are naturally shier than others, or they may be afraid of making a mistake. If your discussion is free and friendly and you show real interest in what other group members think and feel, they will be more likely to speak up. Remember, the more people involved in a discussion, the richer it will be.

5. Guard yourself from answering too many questions or talking too much. Give others a chance to express themselves. If you are one who participates easily, discipline yourself by counting to ten before you open your mouth!

6. Make personal, honest applications and commit yourself to letting God's Word change you.

Ancient World
c.1500-1300 B.C.

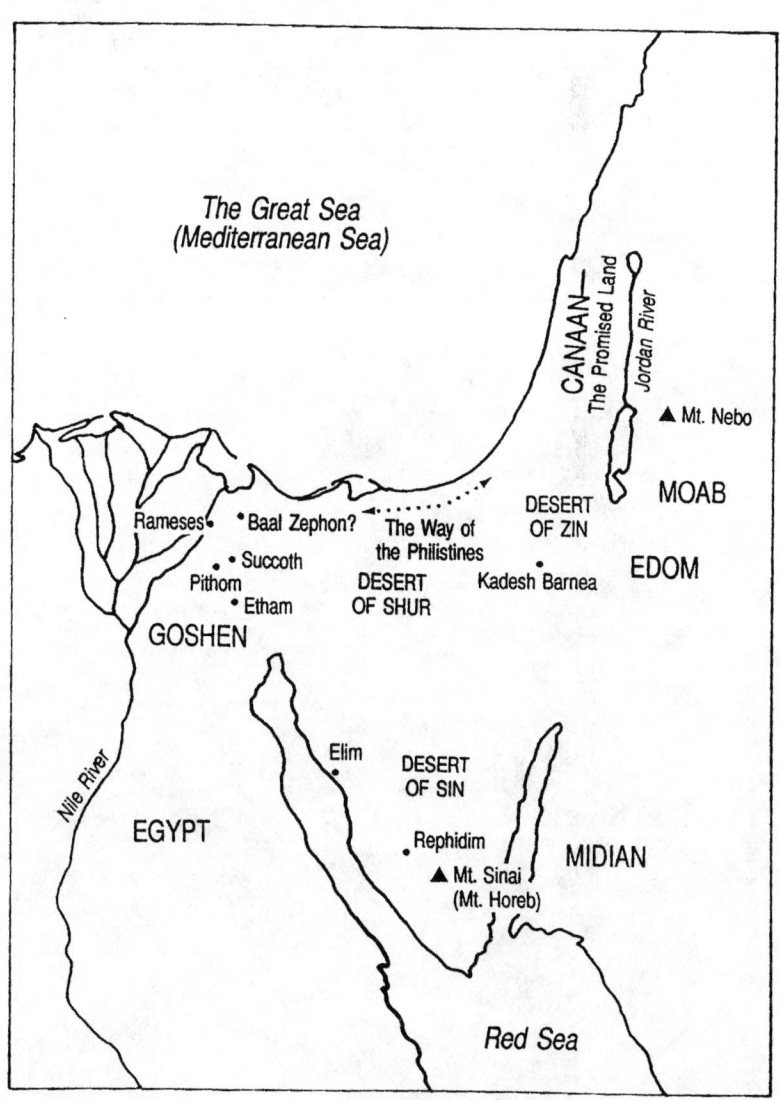

The Great Sea
(Mediterranean Sea)

CANAAN—
The Promised Land

Jordan River

▲ Mt. Nebo

MOAB

Rameses

Baal Zephon?

The Way of
the Philistines

DESERT
OF ZIN

Succoth

DESERT
OF SHUR

Kadesh Barnea

EDOM

Pithom

Etham

GOSHEN

Elim

DESERT
OF SIN

Nile River

EGYPT

Rephidim

MIDIAN

▲ Mt. Sinai
(Mt. Horeb)

Red Sea

The Tabernacle & the Encampment of the Tribes

GOD IS ALREADY ANSWERING

Exodus 1–2; 3:1-15

The check was on the way to you, but you didn't know it. All you knew was that the rent was due and you didn't know how you were going to pay it. You looked at the calendar, saw the dreaded date approaching and tried to figure out how you would explain. And all the while the unexpected envelope was safely making its way through the postal system—being sealed, stamped, mailed, trucked, flown, trucked again, sorted, carried, and finally delivered to your door. God was at work all along—you just didn't know it.

Enslaved in Egypt, the people of Israel cried out to God for release. Had God forgotten them? No, he still cared, and he was beginning to do something to deliver them. But the beginnings of his plan were obscure.

1. Give an example of a situation where God was at work to help you (or someone else) but you had no idea of it until much later.

Read Exodus 1–2.

2. Describe the changes in the Israelites' situation at the time of Moses' birth.

What might the people have been thinking and feeling (1:1-22; 2:23-25)?

3. What people were key in Moses' survival (2:1-10)?

4. From the brief glimpse we get here, what do you know about Moses' life in Egypt (2:1-15)?

What turn did Moses' life take?

Read Exodus 3:1-15.

◆ **5.** Here is the first active indication that God was going to do something about the Israelites' oppression. Describe the setting in which this announcement took place (verse 1).

◆ *Indicates further information in Leader's Notes*

♦ **6.** What do you discover about the heart of God from what he told Moses in verses 7-10?

7. From his responses in verses 2-6, what do you discern about Moses' character?

8. As God spoke the words in verses 7-10, how might Moses' mood have fluctuated?

♦ **9.** What were Moses' objections to being chosen, and how did the Lord counter each of them (verses 11-15)?

♦ **10.** In what ways can you relate to the Israelites' dilemma in verse 7?

11. How was God beginning to help the Israelites in Egypt, even though they didn't yet know about it?

12. What encouragement and hope can you draw from this passage when you face difficult situations?

13. How can this passage affect how you pray for yourself and others during hard times?

THE LORD OVERCOMES DOUBTS

Exodus 4:1–6:12

Have you ever dared complain to the Lord? Maybe you do that all the time; maybe you've done it in the past but not lately; or maybe you consider it unthinkable that a human being would complain to a holy God. Yet we've all experienced times when it felt that God just wasn't doing what we expected or what we needed.

As the story of Exodus continues, Moses and his brother, Aaron, obey the Lord and appeal to Pharaoh for freedom. Immediately it looks as if the whole scheme has backfired. Pharaoh comes down hard on the Israelites, and the Israelites angrily turn on Moses and Aaron. With their promised hope of freedom apparently shattered, Moses turns to the Lord and blurts out his honest feelings.

1. Have you experienced a time in your life when God did not respond as you wanted him to? What did you do?

Read Exodus 4:1-17.

2. The story picks up with Moses still talking with God at the burning bush. What further doubts did Moses express about going to Pharaoh, and how did God successively overcome each doubt?

3. Put yourself in Moses' place for a minute. How would you respond to a task like this? Why?

How has God worked to overcome doubts or fears in your life?

Scan Exodus 4:18–5:21.

4. Moses returned to Egypt and teamed up with his brother, Aaron. What sort of reception did they receive from the Israelites?

5. When Moses asked Pharaoh to release the people, what chain reaction of events followed?

Read Exodus 5:22–6:12.

6. Moses proceeded to complain to God. What was reasonable or unreasonable about his complaints?

♦ **7.** How did God assure the Israelites that he would keep his promise (6:2-5)?

8. The Israelites did not immediately listen to Moses. As a result, what did God tell Moses to do as a next step?

9. Compare and contrast the people's response to Moses with Moses' response to God (6:9, 12). How are they alike? different?

10. What insights into God's character do you glean from his dialogue with Moses here?

♦ **11.** God reminded the Israelites of his past faithfulness. As Christians, what are some things in our corporate church history that reassure us of God's continual care?

12. More specifically, how can God use your own spiritual history to reassure you of his care? (That is, what are some events in your own life that you can recall to remind yourself that God is faithful?)

THE LORD OF POWER

Exodus 7–10

Chicago's Fourth of July fireworks were coming to a close. The grand finale was cascading downward to be quenched in the dark waters of Lake Michigan. Suddenly, crack! A lightning bolt transformed night to day for an instant; then came a *wham!* of thunder. God seemed to be saying, "You think your fireworks are something? Wait till you see what I can do!"

Most people in the crowd probably didn't even think about God in that setting. Even the greatest demonstration of God's power does not necessarily make a non-believer into a believer. But for those who are open to see it, God demonstrates his power every day.

1. What are some ways you have seen God demonstrate his power? (Consider a variety of channels: in nature, in your church, in other people's lives, in your own life.)

Scan Exodus 7–10.

2. Divide into smaller groups of two or three people. As you scan the passage, chart the first nine plagues God sent and answer the following questions together:

What did each plague consist of?

Who was affected?

What was the people's response?

How did Pharaoh respond?

What were the results?

Read Exodus 9:13-21.

3. One reason God brought the plagues on the Egyptians was to persuade Pharaoh to let the Israelites leave Egypt. What other reasons are given (verses 14-16)?

♦ **4.** How could these demonstrations of power result in God's name being "proclaimed in all the earth"?

♦ **5.** What would make the plague of hail a particularly powerful demonstration of the power of God?

6. How was God's mercy shown even as the plague was announced? In other ways?

♦ **7.** What evidence do you see that the plagues were beginning to have the intended effect?

Read Exodus 9:22-35.

8. How was God's sovereignty shown in what was destroyed by the hail and what was spared? Consider both his sovereignty in Israel's history and in the world in general.

9. What did Pharaoh's actions reveal about the sincerity of his repentance? about his true character?

10. Why does even a great demonstration of God's power not completely convince a stubborn person?

11. In what ways does seeing God's power of behalf of his people encourage you?

12. How can you allow what you have experienced of God's power to lead you to deeper holiness and commitment to him?

THE PASSOVER

Exodus 11:1–12:30

What do you use to help you remember things? Some people write big notes to themselves and stick them up in conspicuous places. Others ask friends to remind them of appointments or leave themselves messages on their home answering machines. Some people turn on their computer for their daily calendar to pop up.

Most of us need help remembering the things we should remember. The Israelites were no exception. As God acted for their deliverance, he also gave them a most effective way to recall his faithfulness. That's one purpose of religious rituals—they help us remember what we would otherwise forget.

1. What memory techniques or helps are most effective for you and why?

Read Exodus 11.

2. Describe the events leading up to the final plague on Egypt. Who was involved? What was the tone?

3. As news of the last and most devastating plague began to spread among the Egyptians and the Israelites, what may have been the prevailing mood in each group?

Read Exodus 12:1-23.

4. How were the Israelites specifically instructed to prepare for the Passover (verses 1-13)?

5. What were the requirements for the sacrificial animal (verses 3-5)?

♦ **6.** What significance do you see in the various things that were to be done at this first Passover (verses 5-11)?

7. What positive and negative actions would the Lord himself take (verses 12-13)? Why?

♦ **8.** Moses gave final instructions in verses 21-23. What was to be done with the blood, and why?

Read Exodus 12:24-30.

9. How were the Passover events made into a lasting remembrance to be kept by the people? (Compare Exodus 13:1-16) Why?

10. In what ways is the remembrance of Passover similar to the Christian communion service?

11. What part does communion play in your own experience of worship?

12. Through what other creative means can you celebrate and remember what God has done for you in the past?

THE LORD LIBERATES HIS PEOPLE

Exodus 13:17–14:31

"I don't get it," a friend of ours said. "I stepped out on faith and did what I thought God wanted me to do, and so far it looks like nothing but disaster!"

Is there anything more confusing than having things apparently go wrong when we've obeyed God as best we knew how? That's the distressing situation in which Moses and the Israelites found themselves as they huddled in their encampment by the sea, with deep water on one side and the dust of Pharaoh's approaching army on the other.

1. Have you ever felt stuck in a situation with seemingly no way out? What happened?

Read Exodus 13:17–14:12.

◆ **2.** God did not lead the Israelites along the shorter route through the Philistine country (see map on page 11). What reason did he give for the longer route (13:17-18)?

◆ **3.** What things impress you about God's "guidance system" for the Israelites (13:20-22)?

4. How has God led or guided you recently? How did you know it was God?

5. God had been unmistakably leading the Israelites out of Egypt. Describe the situation in which they now found themselves (14:5-12).

6. How did the Israelites respond to this new emergency?

7. If you had been in the same emergency, what thoughts might have been going through your head? (Compare your hypothetical response with your answer to question 1.)

Read Exodus 14:13-31.

♦ **8.** What command and what assurance did Moses give the people (verses 13-14)?

9. How can Moses' advice still encourage us today when our situation seems hopeless?

10. What different means—natural and supernatural—did God use to intervene and deliver his people (verses 16-22)?

11. God also gave a hint about why he had put the Israelites in this difficult position. What reason did he imply?

12. Have you seen God using a similar "Red Sea" strategy in your own life or someone else's life? Explain.

13. God may not literally part a sea for us, but he is still a God who delivers and frees us, spiritually and physically. What stories of God's deliverance do you have to share?

YIELDING CONTROL

Exodus 16:1-36; 18:9-27

Has it ever happened to you? You were in charge of some big event and you felt responsible for taking care of every detail and making sure it ran like clockwork. Then you got sick or some other emergency came up and you couldn't be there.

And what do you know, the event came off perfectly without you! Other people stepped in, took up the slack and did "your" job quite well. Finding out that we're not 100% necessary, and that we need help, is a humbling—but freeing—experience. Moses had to learn this lesson too.

1. In what areas of life do you especially like to be in charge?

Read Exodus 16:1-36.

2. After all that God had done, why do you think the people responded as they did to the hardships of the desert (verses 1-9)?

3. When the Israelites talked about how good it used to be back in Egypt, what were they forgetting or ignoring?

4. Moses told the Israelites that they were grumbling not against him but against God. When we grumble against circumstances or people in our lives, how could it be said that we are complaining and grumbling against God?

♦ **5.** By what unusual means did God provide for the people in the desert?

Why do you think God put the limits he did on gathering (verses 16-36)?

Read Exodus 18:9-18.

While Moses was in Egypt, his wife Zipporah and his son were staying with his father-in-law Jethro. After the Israelites' escape from Egypt, Jethro accompanied his daughter and grandson to the Israelites' encampment in the desert. Moses reported to Jethro all that God had done.

6. What do we learn about Jethro from his response to Moses' words?

7. Describe what Jethro saw the next day and why it disturbed him.

Read Exodus 18:19-27.

♦ **8.** What was Jethro's method for solving Moses' difficulty?

9. What qualities of character did Moses need in order to accept Jethro's advice?

◆ **10.** What would have been the risks of turning over part of Moses' responsibilities to a group of people who lacked experience?

Beyond the time saved, what were some advantages of Moses' delegating the work to others?

11. In what areas of your life is it difficult for you to relinquish control?

12. Think of the advantages of taking Jethro's advice. What do you need to do to put that advice into action?

GOD'S PERFECT LAW

Exodus 19:1–20:21

Speed Limit 55. Keep Off the Grass. Walk/Don't Walk. No Parking Here at Anytime. No Trespassing. Use Separate Plate for Each Trip to the Salad Bar.

Regulations are everywhere, and few of us welcome them. We complain about them and resist them because we don't like the restrictions they place on our freedom. No wonder it sounds like a contradiction when God says that his laws are designed to give us freedom!

1. Growing up, what part did rules and regulations play in your family? How did you usually react to these?

Read Exodus 19:1-25.

2. The Israelites had wandered for three months and finally stopped in the Sinai Desert. How did God encourage his people as he initiated conversation with them (verses 3-6)?

◆ **3.** Identify all the preparations that had to be made for receiving the law (verses 1-15).

4. What words or phrases would you use to describe the setting where the law was given (verses 16-22)?

Read Exodus 20:1-11.

5. In your own words, relate the essence of each of these first four commandments.

◆ **6.** What is the overarching concern or focus of these four commandments as a whole?

7. What can we discern about the character of God from these commandments?

Read Exodus 20:12-21.

8. Identify the specific areas of life dealt with here.

What is the overall focus of these final six commandments?

9. What further insight do these commandments give you about God's character?

10. Imagine the drama of the scene in verses 18-21. What response did God's presence evoke? Why?

11. People often accuse the Ten Commandments of being too restrictive. Yet the Bible calls God's law *liberating* (see Psalm 119:45 and James 2:12). How would you explain the ways in which the laws of God can be liberating?

12. Which of these commandments have you personally found restrictive? Why?

What has helped bring you around to finding freedom through obedience to God's commands?

LORD OF EVERY PART OF LIFE

Exodus 23:1-19

Some parts of our lives are easy to hand over to God. But for most of us there is a corner or a space—or maybe an elephant-sized room—that we'd like to hold onto and control. What's the area for you? Finances? Personal goals? Sexuality? Your job? Even church?

The Lord stakes his claim on every area of life, not because he wants to spoil our fun but because he wants to transform those areas into something holy and good. But first we have to let them go, acknowledging his ownership of every part of our lives. At Sinai the Lord expanded on the Ten Commandments and gave the Israelites specific instructions about some very close-to-home areas of life.

1. Consider an aspect of your life where you have difficulty yielding to the Lord. What fears or other emotions inhibit you from trusting God with that part of life?

Scan through Exodus 21–22, looking for dominant themes.

2. In what ways does God expand on the Ten Commandments here?

Identify some of the themes and areas of life covered by these more specific laws.

Read Exodus 23:1-9.

3. What common idea(s) do you see running through this section of commands? Discuss.

4. Our culture is very different from the nomadic culture to which these laws were directed. (Most of us don't own a donkey or an ox and don't know anyone who does.) How can the principles of these particular laws be put into practice in our own culture? Discuss some practical examples.

Read Exodus 23:10-19.

5. List the guidelines for remembering the Sabbath. (Compare with Exodus 20:8-11.)

♦ **6.** What benefits were promised for keeping the Sabbath laws?

7. As the people considered obeying these Sabbath commands, what possible concerns may have begun to creep into their minds?

8. What concerns and pressures do we face in trying to keep the Sabbath in our own culture?

♦ **9.** The people were told to celebrate three feasts. How did these feasts demonstrate God's claim on the totality of human life?

♦ **10.** How could we fulfill the intent of these celebrations today within the context of our own Christian community?

11. What will you do this week to celebrate and commemorate God's goodness and faithfulness?

TIME WITH GOD

Exodus 24

It's exciting to be part of a great crowd praising the Lord together; ask anyone who has been in a worship service in a football stadium, arena, or some other vast setting. When thousands of diverse voices mingle into one chorus glorifying God, we realize that as believers we're not alone.

But there are other times we need to be alone—alone, that is, with the Lord himself. Sometimes God takes us out of the crowd so he can capture our full attention. If he needed to do that with his servant Moses, certainly he needs to do it with us.

1. Imagine being actually summoned by God to spend time with him. How do you think you'd react? Why?

As background for this study, scan Exodus 23:20-32.

2. In what ways did the Lord express the depth of his commitment to the future of the Israelites?

Read Exodus 24:1-8.

♦ **3.** Roughly diagram the positioning of the people at the mountain (verses 1-2). What message about God was conveyed by the arrangement?

4. How did the people express their attitude toward God's laws?

♦ **5.** What steps did Moses take in confirming the covenant of God with the people?

Read Exodus 24:9-18.

6. The Hebrew people believed that no one could see God and survive. Yet Moses, Aaron, Aaron's two sons, and the seventy elders went up Mount Sinai and "saw God" (verse 10). How do you account for their willingness to take such a risk?

7. Compare the description in verse 10 with Isaiah 6:1-4, Ezekiel 1:25-28, and Revelation 4:1-6. What impresses you about these descriptions?

8. Consider the time frame of Moses' stay on the mountain with the Lord. What would have been difficult about that lapse of time for Moses? For those waiting for him?

9. If you wish, describe a time when you have spent an extended time apart with God. How did it come about? What did you do?

10. What immediate and/or long-term results have you seen from time spent alone with God?

11. How does your response to God compare with the people's response voiced in verse 7? Pray together that you can respond wholeheartedly as the Israelites did.

"HOLY TO THE LORD"

Exodus 28:1-5, 31-43; 29:1-46

Most of us like a certain degree of ceremony to mark the passages of life. Whether it's a job promotion, the granting of a high school diploma, or the inauguration of a president, we expect some kind of formal observance of the person's new position.

It wasn't that different back in the days of the Israelites. When Aaron and his sons became priests of the Lord, God outlined holy rituals and even special clothing to set them apart for his service. While much of the ancient symbolism is foreign to our culture, the ceremonial importance of what was done still shines through.

1. What ceremony in your life has been meaningful to you, and why?

Read Exodus 28:1-5 and 31-43.

In Exodus 25–27 God gave Moses detailed instructions for the building of the movable tent of worship and the holy articles of worship. Next, God established the priesthood.

2. How were Aaron and his sons to be set apart for a special type of service to the Lord?

3. Identify the various garments described here.

Why do you think God mandated such elaborate and ornate clothing?

4. Suggest how bearing a literal physical remembrance of the Israelites into God's presence might affect Aaron himself.

5. Suggest how knowing that Aaron bore that remembrance might affect the people.

6. In your own experience, what outward symbols have taken the holiness of God out of the abstract and made it more real?

Read Exodus 29:1-46.

7. Enumerate the various steps used in the consecration of Aaron and his sons as priests to the Lord.

◆ **8.** How did the steps of preparation show that Aaron and his sons were inadequate—humanly speaking—to serve as priests?

♦ **9.** What offering was to be made for seven days, and why (verses 35-37)?

10. In connection with the offerings, what promises did God make (verses 42-46)?

11. How did past and future come together in the consecration of Aaron and his sons (note verses 42 and 46)?

12. What things—in creation, in corporate worship, in religious ceremonies—serve to remind you of God's holy presence, as the priests did for Israel?

13. Consider further ways you can daily remind yourself of God's faithfulness to you.

REBELLION, INTERCESSION, AND RESTORATION

Exodus 32

Sometimes God just doesn't move fast enough—at least not as fast as we think he should. When we see problems to be solved and needs to be met, it's hard to understand why God isn't doing something now.

At those frustrating times of waiting, it's tempting to take things into our own hands. We want to construct the solution that God just isn't getting around to providing. Our solutions may take many forms. For Israel, waiting at the foot of Mount Sinai, the form was an idol made of gold.

1. Tell about a time when you seemed to lose the sense of God's presence in your life (or when God seemed very far away). How did the experience affect you?

Read Exodus 32:1-14.

2. List the reasons the people gave for asking Aaron to make them gods.

◆ **3.** What was Aaron's creative response?

Why do you think he complied with the people's demands?

4. How did the people respond to having a new god?

5. With Moses, their representative and leader, absent for forty days, the Israelites felt at a loss. To whom or to what do you sometimes turn when God doesn't seem to be providing the help you expect?

6. In response to Israel's idolatry, what did God propose to do?

7. What does Moses' reply to God say about his character?

8. In Moses' prayer to God in verses 11-13, what were the various steps of the development of his appeal?

9. How can Moses' example further your understanding of interceding for people who have fallen into sin?

Read Exodus 32:15-35.

10. When confronted with the people's sin, Aaron made excuses. In what ways do these resemble typical excuses people make for sin?

11. Moses' response to the people's sin seems harsh by our standards today. Why did he take these actions (verses 25-31)?

What does this passage tell us about the seriousness of sin?

12. How did Moses put his own life on the line for the Israelites (verses 30-33)?

13. Consider people you know who need your intercessory prayers. Using Moses' example, and without revealing to the group things that should be kept private, spend time praying for those people.

A LASTING COVENANT

Exodus 34

Sometimes it seems that nobody keeps promises anymore. From broken marriage vows to useless service contracts to ambitious politicians, people give their word lightly. Often they don't even intend to make good on what they've promised to do. It's refreshing to find someone trustworthy; a person who says "I'll do this"—and then does it.

The Lord is that trustworthy One who keeps his commitments to us. He has made an eternal promise to be faithful to his people, and he has never broken a promise.

1. Who has blessed you by keeping a promise?

Read Exodus 34:1-17.

Earlier in Exodus 33, Moses had despaired at the prospect of being without the Lord's presence. But God assured him that he would never leave, allowing Moses to see God's glory pass by. Then God gave Moses a new task.

2. In anger at the people's idolatry, Moses had smashed the original two stone tablets bearing the Ten Commandments. What do you think was the significance of those tablets being replaced?

◆ **3.** Note God's declarations as he passed before Moses. How do you reconcile the statements in verse 6 with that of verse 7b?

◆ **4.** In his covenant with the people, what did God promise to do (verse 10)? To what end?

♦ **5.** To what extreme measures were the people called to be obedient (verses 13-17)? Why?

6. Why do you think idolatry was such a persistent problem for God's people?

7. In what ways are believers today tempted to depend on something or someone besides the Lord to meet their needs?

What can we do to break down the idols in our lives?

Read Exodus 34:18-35.

♦ **8.** The next requirements of God's covenant with the people included three annual feasts. How could these yearly feasts help them avoid falling back into idolatry?

9. How did Moses' entrance into the camp differ this time (verse 29) from his previous entrance in Exodus 32:19?

How was the people's response different?

10. From verses 29-35, how would you describe Moses' relationship with God?

11. How did that close relationship enable Moses to not compromise God's laws?

12. Which of God's promises have meant more to you over the years? Which ones have meant more to you recently? Why?

Take time to praise the Lord together for his faithfulness to keep his promises.

GIVING BACK TO THE LORD

Exodus 35:1–36:7; 39:32-43

"I wish I could make worship banners like she does . . . or coach softball like him . . . or write music like they do . . . or . . ." It's easy to fall into the trap of envying skills of other Christians. We look at ourselves in comparison and think we don't have much to offer.

Sometimes in the church we elevate performance gifts like music or public speaking while we downplay practical gifts like building and craftsmanship. But there is value in all the various skills God has placed within his church. When we have opportunities to offer our gifts, whatever they are, back to God, then we thrive in our faith.

1. What spiritual gifts or talents do you tend to consider more important than other ones? Why?

Read Exodus 35:1-29.

2. What requirements were set forth for the people who were to make the tabernacle furnishings and provide the materials (verses 2, 5, 10)?

3. Why would these requirements be vital for this task?

4. Consider the gifts and skills represented in this passage. Who do you know who possesses these or similar skills? How are they using them for service?

♦ **5.** What repeated phrases do you observe that describe how the people responded (verses 21-29)?

How does their attitude compare with your own toward giving to the Lord?

Read Exodus 35:30–36:7.

◆ **6.** Obviously there were many artistically gifted people among the Israelites. What set Bezalel, Oholiab, and the other, unnamed craftsmen apart?

7. What "complaint" did the workers make to Moses (36:3-5)?

What do you think motivated the people to give so freely?

8. What inhibits you from giving of your time and talents to the Lord's work?

Read Exodus 39:32-43.

♦ **9.** This passage puts the tabernacle together physically and in the reader's mind. How did Moses react to seeing it all?

Look at the rendering of the tabernacle on page 12. How do you think you would have reacted if you had been there?

10. Think about your own church building and place of worship. How does it display believers' gifts *from* the Lord and *to* the Lord (either material gifts or skills)?

11. Consider your own material resources. What new ways do you see to give to the Lord besides financially?

12. Consider your God-given skills or spiritual gifts. What new avenues can you see for using your abilities for the Lord?

13. Think of someone in your fellowship whose gifts or contributions tend to go unnoticed. How will you affirm that person's gifts this week?

GOD'S PRESENCE FILLS THE TABERNACLE

Exodus 40

We have followed Moses and the children of Israel from Egypt to the wilderness to Mount Sinai. We have watched as God has miraculously delivered his people over and over again. Now as we come to the close of the book of Exodus, we find the Lord faithfully assuring his people that he will always be with them.

How many of us have wished we could see or touch God, just to be sure he was there? Israel had the privilege of watching God's very presence fill the tabernacle they had constructed. But this was no warm fuzzy experience—it was awesome!

1. When have you been overwhelmed by the holiness of God? Tell about it.

Read Exodus 40:1-38.

2. To prepare everything for service, what final things were done in the tabernacle?

3. Describe the final steps of how Aaron and his sons were dedicated to serve the Lord as priests.

4. What impact might all these final preparations have had on the people's attitudes toward the tabernacle and the priests?

5. Finally the magnificent tabernacle was done. Look again at the drawing on page 12. Then, making use of verses 17-33, label each of the nine items in the following diagram of the tabernacle. If there is time, discuss the purpose of each item to be used in worship.

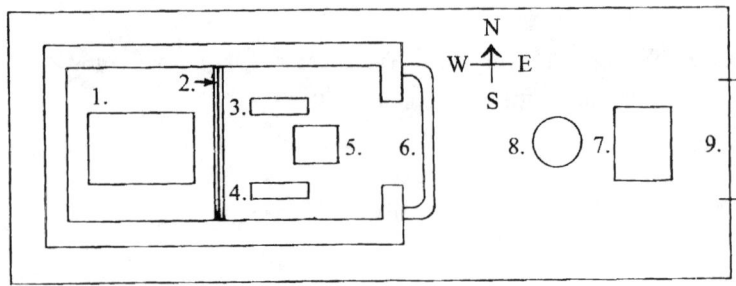

1.

2.

3.

4.

5.

6.

7.

8.

9.

6. When the people had finished setting up the tabernacle, how did the Lord verify that it was his?

7. How have you seen God manifesting himself in your church? (Consider the quiet and obscure manifestations as well as more dramatic ones.)

8. In the New Testament, Christian believers are called God's dwelling place, both individually and corporately (see 1 Corinthians 6:19 and 1 Peter 2:5). What difference does it make in your life to know that you are God's "tabernacle"?

9. As we close our study of Exodus, what main event or themes from this book have fixed themselves in your mind? Why?

10. What have you observed throughout this book study that will help you follow God more closely?

11. We don't have a pillar of cloud or fire to give us guidance, but we do have God's Word and the Holy Spirit to guide us. Israel's problem throughout their history was not discerning what God wanted, but rather their own willingness to obey. What steps can you take now to obey what you believe God wants you to do?

Praise the Lord for always being with you. Pray that you will consistently live in ways that honor his presence.

LEADER'S NOTES

■ **Study 1/God Is Already Answering**

Question 5. The setting was isolated, a good 250 difficult desert miles from the Nile River. Mt. Horeb (Mt. Sinai) would later be the place where God gave the Ten Commandments. It was a rocky, lonely area.

Midian, the home of Jethro, is the far northwest corner of modern Saudi Arabia. (See map on page 11). Moses was tending the family flocks in the southern part of the Sinai Peninsula. "The Midianites were descendants of Abraham through his second wife, Keturah. They were desert-dwellers, so Moses could scarcely have had better preparation for the wilderness journeys with Israel than these years of nomadic life" (*Eerdmans Handbook to the Bible,* pp. 155-156. Grand Rapids, Mich.: Eerdmans, 1973).

Question 6. Notice how the Lord took the initiative to help his people: "I have indeed seen . . .; I have heard them . . .; I have come down to rescue them . . . and to bring them up . . .; I am sending you . . ."

Question 9. "I Am Who I Am" is the divine Name which came to be regarded as so holy that devout Jews would not pronounce it. "It expresses the eternity and immutability of the divine nature, and the faithfulness of God to all his purposes and promises" (William Wilson, *Wilson's Old Testament Word Studies,* p. 259. Peabody, Mass.: Hendrickson Publishers, n.d.).

Question 10. To respond to this question, your situation does not have to be as dramatic as that of the Israelites in slavery. It can be anything which has you "crying out" or "suffering."

■ Study 2/The Lord Overcomes Doubts

Question 7. God makes use of the Israelites' history to assure them of his faithfulness. The previous covenants God had made were with Noah (Genesis 9:8-17) and Abraham (Genesis 15:17-20).

Question 11. Draw on what you know of Christian history in general, the history of your own denomination, the history of your own local church, and the history of your family. Think about how the Lord made use of persecution as well as delivering his people from it. Recall famous and not-so-famous people who stood fast as examples of faith because they found God faithful.

■ Study 3/The Lord of Power

Question 4. See Joshua 2:8-11 for a comparable example of how God's name was proclaimed in other nations as a result of miracles.

Question 5. "Clearly the abilities of several Egyptian gods were again being challenged. Nut, the sky goddess, was not able to forestall the storm; and Osiris, the god of crop fertility, could not maintain the crops in this hailstorm; nor could Set, the storm god, hold back this storm" (John D. Hannah, "Exodus," in *The Bible Knowledge Commentary: Old Testament,* p. 123. Wheaton, Ill.: Victor Books, 1985).

Question 7. Notice that some of the Egyptians took measures to protect their possessions (Exodus 9:20-21). They had learned to expect that if Moses said something would happen, it would happen.

■ Study 4/The Passover

Question 6. "The lamb was to be a year-old male because it was taking the place of Israel's firstborn males who were young and fresh with the vigor of life. The bitter herbs (lettuce and endive are indigenous to Egypt) were to recall the bitter years of servitude (Exodus 1:14), and the unleavened bread was to reflect this event's haste on that first night" (Walter C. Kaiser, Jr., "Exodus," p. 372. *The Expositor's Bible Commentary,* vol. 2, Grand Rapids, Mich.: Zondervan, 1990).

Question 8. In the spreading of the blood of the lamb on the doorpost to save from death, Christians see a foreshadowing of the cross and the blood of Christ which saves us from spiritual death. Peter wrote that we are redeemed "with the precious blood of Christ, a lamb without blemish or defect" (1 Peter 1:19). When John the Baptist saw Jesus, he called out, "Look, the Lamb of God, who takes away the sin of the world!" (John 1:29).

■ Study 5/The Lord Liberates His People

Question 2. The actual route of the Exodus is not known. "The Israelites did not pass along the short section of the Via Maris from Egypt, called in the Bible the 'way of [to] the Land of the

Philistines' . . . ; they [probably] avoided it because of the many Egyptian stations and fortresses along the way. Migdol and Baal-zephon, mentioned at the start of the Exodus (Ex. 14:2; Num. 33:7) are known from Egyptian sources as fortresses at the north-eastern edge of the Delta, and it is thus clear that the Exodus started in the north" (Yohanan Aharoni and Michael Avi-Yonah, *The Macmillan Bible Atlas,* rev. ed., p. 40. New York: Macmillan, 1977).

Question 3. It appears that this particular type of direct, continuing, visible guidance was only for the time of the Exodus, since it is never repeated in Scripture.

Question 8. Compare two similar but later statements of Scripture in Psalm 46:10 and 2 Chronicles 20:17.

■ Study 6/Yielding Control

Question 5. The word *manna* means in Hebrew "What is it?" (Exodus 16:15, 31).

Question 8. "Jethro's solution to this lengthy process, which was wearing out both people and leader (v.18), was to give Moses that portion of the work that involved a twofold office: (1) an advocate on behalf of the people (v.19) and (2) an interpreter on behalf of God to teach the people (v. 20). Jethro warned that his plan needed to be executed only if God was pleased with this advice. . . . Moses' work was to be supplemented with additional help" *(Expositor's Bible Commentary,* p. 413).

Question 10. Without the burden of deciding all of the disputes, Moses would have more time to devote to the more difficult cases. By sharing his leadership, Moses was preparing others for leadership roles in the community.

■ Study 7/God's Perfect Law

Question 3. "The necessary process of ritual purification, or setting apart for God, included the washing of garments . . . and temporary abstention from sexual intercourse. . . . This was not because the latter was considered as wrong in any way, but because, by Mosaic law, it required ceremonial bathing for religious purification as an aftermath. . . . Nevertheless we may compare Paul's words, allowing temporary abstention that Christians may devote themselves to prayer (1 Cor. 7:5)" (R. Alan Cole, *Tyndale Old Testament Commentaries,* p. 146. Downers Grove, Ill.: Inter-Varsity Press, 1973).

Question 6. Compare the group's responses to questions 5 and 7 with Jesus' summary of the Law in Mark 12:28-31.

■ Study 8/Lord of Every Part of Life

Question 6. Allowing fields to rest or lie fallow is an accepted farming practice used in many parts of the world. Today the use of fertilizers and pesticides has largely replaced this practice.

Question 9. For further information on the feasts, compare with Deuteronomy 16:1-17.

Question 10. Though many of us don't live in an agricultural society working directly with land, we still are recipients of God's blessings and totally dependent on his generosity for all we have.

■ Study 9/Time with God

Question 3. Note that Exodus 24 continues the narrative from Exodus 20:21. The story "was temporarily interrupted for the contents of the 'Book of the Covenant' (20:22–23:33). . . . Moses and his aides were to ascend . . . the mountain after the actions mentioned in vv. 3-8 were completed" (*Expositor's Bible Commentary,* p. 448).

Question 5. The early sacrificial system which God set up for the Israelites was a foreshadowing of the coming eternal covenant through Christ's blood. Compare Hebrews 9:11-22.

■ Study 10/"Holy to the Lord"

Question 8. They were consecrated by God (Exodus 29:1, 44). The sacred garments symbolized the fact that they were set apart by God's choice (verses 5-8). They had to be washed (verse 4). They were anointed with oil (verse 7). Sacrifices were made for them (verses 10-14).

Question 9. The Hebrew word for *atonement* means "to cover, to cover sin, or to secure the sinner from guilt and punishment. . . . This word conveys the idea both of pacification of wrath, and of the covering of transgression, but does not seem to express of itself the idea of full and adequate satisfaction for sin" *(Wilson's Old Testament Word Studies,* p. 24). For further insight on the incompleteness of the Old Testament sacrifices and their fulfillment in Christ's sacrifice, refer to Hebrews 10:1-18.

■ Study 11/Rebellion, Intercession, and Restoration

Question 3. The civilizations surrounding the Israelites were polytheistic, worshiping multiple gods. Israel had been chosen by God to become a monotheistic people worshiping one God—a radical departure from other cultures. Obviously, temptations to polytheism were everywhere.

Regarding the golden calf, it's interesting to note that a silver calf idol was discovered in the summer of 1990 during an archeological dig at the Canaanite city of Ashkelon. "The bull or calf symbolism expressed in metal and other media was associated with El or Baal, leading deities in the Canaanite pantheon" (Lawrence E. Stager, "When Canaanites and Philistines Ruled Ashkelon," *Biblical Archaeology Review,* p. 28. March/April 1991).

■ Study 12/A Lasting Covenant

Question 3. A human analogy, though an imperfect one, of God's declaration of his character here is that of parents both praising and disciplining their children. Both are expressions of the parents' love.

Question 4. In Genesis 15, God had made a covenant with Abraham (Abram), promising to give this land to his descendants. In that covenant there were no requirements on Abraham's behavior. Now, at Sinai, God commanded obedience in order for the other peoples to be defeated and for Israel to possess the land.

Question 5. Compare this incident with Gideon's pulling down of the altar to Baal and the Asherah pole in Judges 6:25-27. The Lord was asking for the destruction of anything which competed with him as an object of worship. He had already warned the Israelites at Sinai that he was "a jealous God" (Exodus 20:5).

Question 8. The feasts would remind the people of their miraculous escape from Egypt and the Lord's provision for them in the harvest. They would serve as an annual reminder that they were dependent on the Lord for their freedom, their destiny as a nation, and their daily food.

■ Study 13/Giving Back to the Lord

Question 5. It's interesting to note that in Exodus 32 the people had freely given their gold to Aaron for an idol. Now, with changed hearts, they willingly brought their gold again to honor God.

Exodus 35:22 mentions that they presented their gold as a "wave offering." This was part of the larger ritual of a "fellowship offering" which expressed gratitude and symbolized peace with God (see Leviticus 7:28-34).

Question 6. Refer to Exodus 31:1-6 for God's earlier stamp of approval on these craftsmen.

Question 9. Exodus 36–39 give further details about the items the craftsmen built for the tabernacle. These chapters are similar to the descriptions we read previously in Exodus 25–30. While chapters 25–30 give God's instructions through Moses for constructing the items, chapters 36–39 relate how the Israelites carried through and obeyed, making each item as directed.

WHAT SHOULD WE STUDY NEXT?

To help your group answer that question, we've listed the Fisherman Guides by category so you can choose your next study.

TOPICAL STUDIES

Angels, Wright
Becoming Women of Purpose, Barton
Building Your House on the Lord, Brestin
The Creative Heart of God, Goring
Discipleship, Reapsome
Doing Justice, Showing Mercy, Wright
Encouraging Others, Johnson
The End Times, Rusten
Examining the Claims of Jesus, Brestin
Friendship, Brestin
The Fruit of the Spirit, Briscoe
Great Doctrines of the Bible, Board
Great Passages of the Bible, Plueddemann
Great Prayers of the Bible, Plueddemann
Growing Through Life's Challenges, Reapsome
Guidance & God's Will, Stark
Heart Renewal, Goring
Higher Ground, Brestin

Integrity, Engstrom & Larson
Lifestyle Priorities, White
Marriage, Stevens
Miracles, Castleman
One Body, One Spirit, Larson
The Parables of Jesus, Hunt
Prayer, Jones
The Prophets, Wright
Proverbs & Parables, Brestin
Satisfying Work, Stevens & Schoberg
Senior Saints, Reapsome
Sermon on the Mount, Hunt
A Spiritual Legacy, Christensen
Spiritual Warfare, Moreau
The Ten Commandments, Briscoe
Who Is God? Seemuth
Who Is Jesus? Van Reken
Who Is the Holy Spirit? Knuckles & Van Reken
Wisdom for Today's Woman: Insights from Esther, Smith
Witnesses to All the World, Plueddemann
Worship, Sibley

BIBLE BOOK STUDIES

Genesis, Fromer & Keyes
Exodus, Larsen
Job, Klug
Psalms, Klug
Proverbs: Wisdom That Works,
  Wright
Jeremiah, Reapsome
Jonah, Habakkuk, & Malachi,
  Fromer & Keyes
Matthew, Sibley
Mark, Christensen
Luke, Keyes
John: Living Word, Kuniholm
Acts 1-12, Christensen
Paul (Acts 13-28), Christiansen
Romans: The Christian
  Story, Reapsome
1 Corinthians, Hummel
Strengthened to Serve
  (2 Corinthians),
  Plueddemann
Galatians, Titus & Philemon,
  Kuniholm
Ephesians, Baylis
Philippians, Klug
Colossians, Shaw
Letters to the Thessalonians,
  Fromer & Keyes
Letters to Timothy, Fromer &
  Keyes
Hebrews, Hunt
James, Christensen
1 & 2 Peter, Jude, Brestin
How Should a Christian Live?
  (1, 2 & 3 John), Brestin
Revelation, Hunt

BIBLE CHARACTER STUDIES

David: Man after God's Own
  Heart, Castleman
Elijah, Castleman
Great People of the Bible,
  Plueddemann
King David: Trusting God for
  a Lifetime, Castleman
Men Like Us, Heidebrecht &
  Scheuermann
Moses, Asimakoupoulos
Paul (Acts 13-28), Christensen
Ruth & Daniel, Stokes
Women Like Us, Barton
Women Who Achieved for
  God, Christensen
Women Who Believed God,
  Christensen

Printed in the United States
by Baker & Taylor Publisher Services